To my daughter Laurynn, you changed my life forever, for the better.

I love you eternally.

A river never sings the same song twice.

The canyons, carved through bones and sandstone,
Echo with dying storms and coyote calls
In the silent aftermath of withering centuries.
There are moments
When this choruses of solitude
Beneath bruising shades,

This whispering refrain
Before footprints faded,
And her throat was flush with Spring.

GHOST

OF A

RIVER

THOMAS HINDS

Ghost of a River

Copyright © 2022 by Thomas Hinds

Published by ©Hindsight Musings

First Edition

thomashindsmedia.com

Cover art: Dan Coe (dancoecarto.com)

Cover design: Susi (creativeblueprintdesign.com)

Editing: Lessie (mindandmint.com)

Page layout & formatting: Ines (inesbookformatter.com)

ISBN 979-8-9868500-2-3 (paperback)

ISBN 979-8-9868500-1-6 (eBook)

CONTENTS

I. HEADWATERS

GHOST OF A RIVER

There was a time when this jagged river

Cut through the dusty valley

Singing with the voices of a thousand warriors.

Day and night, it echoed

Through these canyons of tall grass,

Overflowing with life.

Cottonwoods glimmering green,

Pinons proud and strong,

Were footprints of angels

Eras before strangers' spilt blood in the rising sands.

A melody called every creature,

Bringing life where it precariously hung

By the thinnest, fraying threads,

Yet slowly the watermark receded.

The ancient trees withered in the distance

As the canyon turned from lush to meager temperament

And surrounding life learned a new harmony.

As the meandering song slowed to an unrecognizable hum

Caught in the shifting winds,

A descending, familiar echo

Paid reverence to this ghost through the passage of time.

Still, the river reminisces on nights beneath a waning moon.

She smiles in her ever-blossoming way,

Dancing in and out of shadows cast by wandering clouds

As they sail east for new songs and

The birth of tomorrow's rhythm.

Although a barren view,

The ghost continues to sing,

Bringing life to the lifeless.

NEVER FELT THE FALL

Over rivers
Gliding on tattered wings of hope,
We believe in tomorrow

Even with split lips and swollen eyes.
The world is a tumble from a tree;
Funny how we never felt the fall.

Winter's scars
  Beneath our skin,
    Rosy cheeks,
      Numbing fingers,
        Blooming spring,
        Wide eyes,
      Cleansing rain,
          Summer heat,
        Glowing smile,
          Endless sand,
      Cobalt sky,
        Longest of days,
       Alive with possibilities,
      Cascading foliage,
    Nature's fireworks,
  Dimming days,
Fading hearts...

Funny how we never felt the fall.

DANGEROUS KIND

Two Hearts and an open road,
Sharing everything in their souls,
It's old Tom Waits and Heart of a *Saturday Night*.

Murmuration over cottonwood trees,
Rearview mirror and your rosary,
Swear to God you knew I'd see the light.

Windows wide open,
Time flew by,
Found your heart in the arms of the dangerous kind.

Underneath powerlines,
Full moon perched on copper wire,
I never told a story you couldn't see straight through.

Casualties of a fevered youth,
Summer greens and winter blues,
It's funny, I never lost my taste for you.

Dangerous,
Desperate,
Restless,
Reckless.

We never found our way back home,
How could you and I have known,
There in the dark, we knew we felt the truth.

A POSTIVE TETHER

I've seen her, hand on the Devil's throat,

Stand before Death's gaze and never back down.

There is a strength in her calm;

She's been to hell and back

With the burn marks to prove it.

That is where I failed...

I believed she needed me.

When she chose me as a place of comfort,

I was cold as stone,

No sign of shelter from a self-proclaimed teddy bear,

No compassion from a once-tender heart.

I stood over her tear-stained cheeks.

While she rested in her resolve

I wept,

A proud man

Who thought he worth her time,

And found he was nothing

But everything wrong with this world.

Colder than necessary,

I showed no warmth.

The biggest fool of all,

Wrapped up in my own selfishness

With no clue how to be what she needs:

A kind word,

A gentle touch,

A positive tether.

THE TASTE OF THE WILD

Remember you said

I tasted wild,

Like I'd never settle down.

How does that turn to roadkill?

Skipped beats and forgotten scars

Return to calm shores

They once believed were laid to rest.

The ghosts haunted the shallows,

Then slipped deeper

Into places untouched for lifetimes.

Push harder, grip tighter on the sails

About to swing and change direction;

Harbors only give shelter for so long.

I don't deserve half the kindness I've been shown,

But I am grateful for every ounce.

Even when I was cold as winter soil,

I had a feeling you would be the death of me.

Always hoped I'd go first

Because I'm a coward in some ways.

Even if admitting it leaves

A bitter taste in my mouth,

It's honest.

I'm not here for kudos or pageantry

Or competing for the best worst story,

But this tragedy I carved out

Has too many bloody hands to count,

And I take responsibility for them all.

I am my own nemesis;

Most days I wish I could cut the power

To the overthinking part of my surging brain.

Hasn't happened yet,

But maybe one more landmine

And I'll find the catalyst to waking up.

Maybe.

MY POETRY

This is my poetry:

The connection between constellations
And the freckles on my skin;
Countless variations
Of where I could be and where I stand,
Each path leading to a thousand more steps.
Why worry about chapters I never wrote
Or endings that came too soon?
I am the poison,
The slow death I swallow with morning coffee,
And it is freeing
To see the end from the beginning.
No matter how we fight,
Train,
Strain,
Or try to alter our storyline,
The end is still there waiting
Like a Christmas we didn't foresee.
Isn't that the beauty of the journey?
Doesn't the knowledge that life is fleeting
Make us savor what we are given?
It should help us be better humans,
Be a little kinder and
Gentler in our breaking moments;
Instead of inflicting the most damage possible,
We should show love and a softer touch.

Maybe it will be seen and felt

Long after we fall forever asleep;

Maybe our impact is what gives shine to

Stars, lightyears away, and

Why we can't help but look up

On the darkest nights

And wishfully sigh.

WINDOW VIEWS

Lives lived

Standing at a window

In a room

Overlooking the splintered valley.

On the stained wall

Is a painting of a picture—

The version of us

You believed we should have been.

I tried to get the copper taste

Out of my mouth

After you spat a bloody version of my name

When you closed the door one last time.

I cannot live passionless;

My tongue stalled in the jilted moment,

Subconsciously unconscious.

I do wish I had more words ready,

Because the sting of your admitted regret

Was a boot heel in my chest.

Now, I'm sleeplessly trying to

Keep this all from turning to ash,

Sinking into the muck.

I've burned Atlanta down

A thousand times before,

Yet this self-imploding tragedy

Walked upright through graffitied cathedral alleyways.

Smokey haze and cinder

Settled into my lungs as I sang,

Lamented the lost summer rain.

I returned to our room with everything unsaid

Like a snare in the doorway;

Perhaps this called for a little mental bloodletting

As I faded in your rearview.

Maybe if I said you only went out for a smoke,

A new bottle of rye,

I could string together

Some semblance of the apology you deserved,

But the silence still hangs like a rusty blade.

These scars never heal

From the infection of my soul.

WITHER

Withering is

A graceful way to fade;

The word paints

A beautiful demise for anything mortal.

Whether the rage of summer heat

Or the transition to needling cold,

With withering comes the chance of rebirth.

The only way to live is to die

And move past our grip

On everything we cannot control.

We try to hold the tide

But it will always change the shoreline.

The ebb and flow of people,

Places,

Names, and

Faces can change in the flutter of a lash or a

Dilating pupil in life's evolving landscape.

Shutter the focus,

Draw the details narrow then wide.

We are the vibration of sunlight and rain,

Thunder growl and roaring surf;

Let the rust gather when we sleep forever,

Shrouded in the dust that remains

Eternal in our bed of rebirth

Where we blossom in the withering.

MOTHS

Moth to a naked flame

Dipped in paraffin and honeysuckle,

A river of time through an open wound.

Dulled brilliance

Dimmed catastrophe in a sagging shroud

Pointed at the miles of sun-dried bones

We narrowly avoided.

Shake off the downpour;

Step into the feeling of summer

As crystals sink into our skin.

Where have we been?

What the hell have we done?

Bruises yellow as they dissipate

And I am hung by my own aging hands.

Swallow me,

I may be the cure

But I may be the cancerous catalyst for breaking hearts.

Unintentional bloodletting

Is still the start of another scar.

Rub the ointment into the laceration,

Catch your breath;

Adrenaline will ease the burning.

Paths of thistle

Tearing at the rags around these feet,

Soaked in life and living.

I am not a commodity, or am I?

Bought and sold

By learning to accept the very thing I despise,
My name spoken in a broken shiver.

No fear
When you face everything head-on
Is the pill I digest daily.
If there were no fear,
Would we know we were alive?
If peace were eternal,
Would we hunger for more

Than the mediocrity marinating our souls?
Some days I believe you take my melancholy
As infinite sadness
And not in the way of Smashing Pumpkins.
I'm sober,
Sobering to some,
But passionate...

Flawed more than I admit.
Hell, who am I kidding?
I admit to many flaws,
And it's still half the truth.
A soft touch
With a tendency to show more mercy
Than anyone deserves

To everyone but myself.
You can't judge me
When I've already sentenced myself
To temporary shelters.
Solitude has a way of showing you
Shadows you have never seen before.

HIDE THE LIGHT

I hide my light just out of view;

Certain creases in my soul

Will flash from time to time

With no rhyme or reason

For how or why.

I do understand my pursuit

Puts me in places exposed

More than a 9-to-5,

And the language of my heart has a way

Of tangling my head in concertina wire,

Especially when I'm tripping over my own feet,

My own tongue, and my own humanity.

Not necessarily a bad thing—

The Achilles of manhood,

The chink in the armor,

The blind spot we tell ourselves we've considered.

Yet, here we lie again,

Face down on a familiar stretch of pavement,

Road rash exposed in a smokey reflection.

I'm not sure anyone has ever known me;

I've spent all my life learning everyone else's stories,

Mine seems mundane and unworthy,

Fading ink on dulling skin.

Tattoos are below the surface,

Burning blooms of *could've been*,

Beautiful bruises shifting shades

To hopeful outcomes until reality rears its ugly head.

So, dance while the music plays,

Those moments were real and never fake.

I have no way to avoid the fields of daisies

Covering the landmines of self-destruction;

I'd post a sign, but they are ever evolving

And never appear the same way twice.

Maybe there should be a better word

For this sort of fuckery.

Would love to blame it on someone else,

But I own my sins,

Embrace my scars,

Here I am—

Better from a distance,

More appealing through a telescope.

Maybe I've been the Supernova this whole time.

MASTER WORK

Rainy days should be

Holed up in a hotel room,

Tangled sheets and writing poetry

On blushing skin with black ink

From a ball point pen.

See how many freckles disappear

Beneath fingerprints painting the story of us,

A portrait of possibility.

Maybe the dream slips by,

But we smile in the melancholy;

Sometimes the bitter makes it a little sweeter,

Who am I to say?

All I know is here I sit

With another Not-An-Old-Fashioned,

Debating the reason

Distance could change the impact

On an ever-expanding universe.

How an inebriated mind works,

Or at least mine does—

Bigger thoughts,

Sharper blades,

No one can cut me deeper than my own tongue.

How did I get to this bar

When just an hour ago

I was playing Van Gogh

With a palette of lugubrious hues?

Sue me for not wanting to

Use melancholy twice in one piece.

I am beginning to believe

I am built for a staggering demise,

Weaving of diluted tapestries.

I should have stayed

But knew it would hurt more six months from now,

So I hit the highlights

With brighter shades of who I wished I were.

I wish I had smaller dreams and

Could swallow 9-to-5

Until I was too old to give a shit,

But no chance.

I am built for hurricanes and flash floods,

Desert summers and aching winters.

Hate me for what you thought I was,

But love me for who I really am:

Me.

MELANCHOLY

My melancholy

Always looked better in soft light

Away from the jagged shadows of summer.

I breathed into the healing spring sky

Solitary songs

Calling like invisible tendrils

Clinging to the meat of my soul.

Let this grey wash over the dreams

We sacrificed in the darkness

Try to appear heroic in some way.

There is no wrong answer now,

Just a split moment to adapt and grow,

Evolve and bloom.

We are the aftermath

Of where we might have been,

Who we are, and where we started.

No apologies,

No excuses,

Believe in your path,

Your step,

Your heart...

It only needs your faith.

Cover your path with passion

And the sea will divide beneath your feet

FEATHERED WINGS

With spring comes the birds;

Songs, like chicks,

Hatch within the nest of my chest.

My heart has shown patience

In warming these thoughts,

Dreams, and visions.

I have wandered this country

With the words of poet and troubadour alike;

They feed my soul and steady my weight,

Preparing me for the rising heat of summer.

Blossoming sunrise

Shows me the melodies I've missed,

And wraps itself around each note

Like a lover after a late night's revelry.

Needing to release the doves

Into the dawning day,

Seeing the sun split the darkness with eyes closed,

Mouths open, and skin wet with heat.

Passionate poems written on our bones,

Take flight when the time comes,

The sky alive with feather-fluttering symphonies.

Angels...perhaps,

Mortal...definitely,

Bolt into the blue

Like forever may be attainable.

As far as we know, the wave will roll

Into the ascending moon,

Dancing on the ripple we create,

Becoming immortal.

THE NEXT STEP

A brushstroke across the waning skyline

Is the last breath of a dying day,

A day that slipped through careless fingers.

Sometimes we cannot save the marrow,

It is elusive.

Blink, and it's gone,

Exhale, and gravity is lost.

We fight to keep the remaining daylight;

Is this as difficult as it sounds?

Maybe, with a tall glass of overthinking

To chase the track record

Of weak moments and poor choices

Waiting in the shadows.

Deep roots

Work towards brighter blooms,

Sweeter sins, and better tomorrows.

Let the brush sweep the night in,

We will live another day,

Dream another dream,

Pray another prayer.

Finish strong and leave the world

Asking questions with no answers.

There's still enough change for cab fare,

Strength is in the next step.

NOSTALGIA

Nostalgia is

The hours spent

In the back

Of an Oldsmobile Cutlass station wagon

Memorizing passing landscapes

As towns appear and fade.

The feeling in my stomach:

Anticipation.

Late-70s has a Polaroid color scheme

And I am washed out

In blurred fingers

Caught in the corner

Of underdeveloped pictures

We shook for hours on end.

Family trips were never enough

To keep us together.

Seems no matter how far we traveled,

We would eventually

Return home

To that quiet street,

Pitched roof,

And lonely yellow kitchen.

Years spent patching holes

In the jeans of a boy

Too free to break with belts and a baptism;

The road was caught in his dreamer's soul,

Unrepentant and wide awake,

Now in the rearview.

Maybe the twilight will satisfy

The wanderlust blooming inside his chest.

The road before him is endless

And the golden hue left behind

Still whispers in quiet tones

From places where songs begin.

Melodies born like a first kiss and

A last look at everything you've ever known.

Memories are rarely what we remember,

But they will be the thread

Telling the story

Of everything after.

EXPECTATION

Expectations are shady bastards.
I have long conversations with myself
About how they are a killer
I can't afford to keep in my pocket,
Yet somehow, they become entangled
In the forgotten lint and change.
Could be the smallest things
Fester just under the skin—
A strange splinter
In your finger.
When it appears,
It's painful,
Infected,
And you can't look away.
You end up ruminating
Because you weren't as ready
As you believed yourself to be.
The smallest of things
Will blindside you every time
And leave you with a wound
Nothing more than self-inflicted ego.
How could they not do this or be that?
Am I not worth the time?
Needless heartache and
Scars of imaginary blades
That never brushed your skin.
Could be they never felt the way
You do or did.

Could be they felt it all,

But to protect themselves

They gave you every excuse to walk away

In hopes you would see

How this love isn't worth the effort.

Maybe you didn't see in their eyes,

This heart was temporary shelter in a difficult time.

Maybe you were just enough

To give them hope in the future

And finding golden moments along the journey.

The hardest part

Is remembering I'm built for the temporary.

Sometimes I forget my place

And dream about forever,

Although love will always be

Mere tastes of timelessness.

BLIND SPOTS

We always have a blind spot

In our perspective,

Something we can't see

Until we have it all "figured out,"

The presumption of having it together

When we don't know a damn thing.

Maybe it's the era when I grew up,

But every memory is reflected

In a warm Polaroid or a shitty 8mm reel.

I find comfort in these playbacks,

But sometimes I tend

To enshrine them with more golden hues

Than were really there,

Creating a shadowed truth

Into something resembling fantasy.

I need to reframe some of the illusion

Into a black and white display of cutting truths.

Reality is always needed;

Something to help me

Question things a little more,

And push the misinterpretation

Until I get it through this thick skull.

I don't claim to be the only one,

This is not the first time

I've found the real story in hindsight;

Sometimes we want something too much.

Love shouldn't cause anxiety,

And it is never a one-way street.

If it wasn't meant to be,

Then you cannot mold the ending

Into a movie with a terrible plot

And a punch-drunk character.

Breathe,

Let the change happen

And embrace the road you take;

It is yours to walk.

Be a driver,

Not a passenger.

RUPTURED HEART

I'm beginning to believe
My ruptured heart
Wakes up early each day
To leave a whispered good morning in your ear.

It has a selfish way,
Of not listening,
Opening in the face possible devastation,
Fearless in the way it leaps from my chest.
No parachute,
No bones to break,
Only walls to tear down
And loose the rubble in the shattering.
The winds of time
Clear a path between here
And where we are meant to be.

Scary, I know,
Yet what is meant to stand,
What is destined to be lost
In the arid Sahara
Wrapped around bones,

What was once everything,
Is now merely shadows under streetlight
Waving in the predawn exhale

Where the sugar rush fades,
Smiles smeared
Across familiar sheets and off-white pillowcases.

Don't worry, hope will linger,

A spark and flicker,

The recollection of the neon hum

Cradling hands through empty city streets

Alive with electric gaslight.

The sound of scraping shoes,

Low spoken conversation,

Comfortable laughter,

The anticipation,

The quiet goodnight left on bitten lips.

These bruises on ripened fruit,

Sweeter than honey,

Are Nature's candy-coated resurrection.

SEA FOAM

Sea foam and brine,
Seaweed like a bloodstain
On stones as old as time.
Waves roll out and in;
In death,
In birth,
Sweeping the sand clean.
Sun sinking
In blushes and bruises,
Paints the line of clouds.
I am aging too quickly
To realize my own fate;
Seagulls above me
Would pick my bones clean
If given the chance.

They have this down,
Knowing their lot in life,
Playing to their strengths.

Meanwhile,
I keep revealing my weaknesses
Like a damn badge of courage,
Yet we both know
A heart is destined to feel
Only so many waves
Before it disappears into
The dark deep
Out beyond the horizon.

WATER'S PULL

You need the water.

Does it whisper your name as you sleep

The way I have?

The waning and waxing of the lunar pull

Has carved your story

Into the belt of Orion—

The heart-wrenching tragedy of love and loss,

The warrior of the winter skyline.

You have unknowingly become

And have yet to recognize the warpaint

In the mirror's gaze.

It's okay to love yourself,

To weep in the beauty pain can create,

The art of life is an evolving canvas.

When we look through unfiltered eyes,

We see ripples over rainbow stones.

Life is tidal

When you breathe with trembling confidence.

Most times we are last to see

How far we've traveled, for fear of looking back.

The distance of time...immeasurable,

And the impact of souls...incalculable.

No matter what the seasons bring,

You need to know

I am blessed I had you in my life,

Your impact

Resonates inside this heart.

SPARKS OF MOONLIGHT

We collided unintentionally

Like sparks of moonlight

Filtering through needles of evergreen.

Our trajectory evolved into a breath-held orbit,

At least from where I stood.

The fragments left beneath my skin

Are waiting for an echo.

The repeat of a beat

Skips like stones on a frozen lake,

A reflection of lunar gravity,

Near weightless fingerprints left behind.

My core has been breached

And words slip from this drying pen,

Hopeful, yet hesitant.

Love is always like peeling layers of skin,

The exposure of something sacred

Not meant for the eyes of the world.

What the eyes cannot see is

Raw and scary as hell.

But we are only seen by one soul,

Felt by one heart;

A one-time only moment,

Meant to be shared

But never recaptured.

Connections that last a lifetime

Find new moments over and over,

Otherwise, we become lost in the disconnect,

Memories etched like scars across our life lines.

All are meant to be a lesson which
Too many never quite grasp.

DREAMSCAPE

I recognized the view as if from a dream,

A past life,

Perhaps it was a bit of both.

A bird's-eye perspective,

Fishing boats with sleepy sunrises,

Espresso-flavored exhales

Rolling out like morning fog,

The second coming of angels

We tried to name

In the war of attrition,

Attention given to understated indulgences.

You were above the fishermen

And their Italian prayers to saints lost in the cataclysm,

Tearing the curtain between God and man,

The tongue of the Creator

With whom we were desperate to make peace

When tranquility was only to be found

In letting go.

The foundation we rose from,

The universal Truth:

To give unselfishly with the heart.

Charity and kindness are the road

That leads to happiness,

A more fulfilling journey.

As I look over the face of this water,

Feeling its inherent calm,

I think about the times

I was rescued from drowning

In the very place you now rest.

II. THE FLOODPLAIN

RUN FOR THE ROSES

Roses run along the Ohio River,

Bridges left miles behind.

Sunsets and sunrises

Share the same palette,

Yet are never the same.

The roar of a crowd,

The roll of liquid songs smoothing stone,

Cutting clay

With the rain, the water rises.

The easing drought

Exposes the century's watermark.

How many indigenous hearts

Carved those lost memories?

Bloodstains,

Birthmarks,

Broken arrows,

Now a blushing cityscape.

Seasons of millennia,

Decades by the score,

Clouds whisper and rage.

The blossoming September

Arrives like the first kiss of autumn.

Here we sit,

Dreaming of the biting winter's howl.

3AM TINKERINGS

My soul could feel the salt in the air,

The sea's tidal pull,

How the jagged coast,

So raw and vicious,

Could soothe the pieces of me

That resemble bottles broken on road signs.

I'm not sure I can forgive myself

For my blindness,

For causing pain,

Unintended or not.

I would break my own bones

Before I would want to cause an ounce of hurt;

I would quietly excuse myself from someone's life

Before I'd be the cause of their pain.

At least then I can be the bad guy,

A part I've played throughout my life.

So, go on and find a way to heal,

I'll be over here cheering

For you to get all your heart wants.

After the karmic hell you've been through,

You deserve it.

LEFTOVER PIECES

I had no right to believe

I was going to change

The way the wind blew.

The nerve of me

To step into a space

That never felt right.

I am too raw,

Unbridled, and wild

For the world you linger in,

So I will sketch the setting sun

Fading into the rolling ocean,

And feel you disappear like cigarette smoke.

When you leave, there's a box by the door,

Feel free to take what you need.

I can piece the remaining parts

Into some semblance of a working heart;

I just hope what you remember

Helps get you through.

THE LETTING GO

Did you feel that?

I said your name

And let go of everything

I believed to be true.

I saw the disregard first-hand,

The twist of reality

To make me feel like

I didn't want any of this.

Fact is, I did;

I wanted it all

And it could have been something unwritten,

But now it's marked out in bloody ink.

I'm grateful for the new tattoo,

For the songs,

For the prose,

For the dance we ended on the edge of madness.

I need that from time to time—

To dangle my limbs from the 18th floor balcony,

The rush of the unexpected

Jolting through my gut into my chest.

Like you said,

You weren't sure that fire existed anymore,

Flames that consumes moments

And set them in stone.

I bow to you

And twirl you in a new direction;

I never expect it to be a season,

Yet it always is.

And I'm still here,

I'm still me,

Just a new set of melodies

Laid over a new set

Of self-inflicted wounds.

I would never dream of implicating

A second set of fingerprints

Inside these lungs.

I stare into the predawn sky

And see there never was a sunrise;

It was everything you needed,

To put away the past.

A taste of salt on your tongue,

To fuck me like you hate me,

Quite simple in the end.

Less messy to keep it carnal,

Can't muck it up too awful bad.

Cheers to the silence,

Cheers to the exhale,

Cheers to the mountain

Left in the shadow of doubting.

It's always worth the pain.

BLESSED LUNGS

The miles and hours pile together

As the sun fades from the sky.

I replay moments of my life,

They fly by in blurs of neon

And shimmering, whitewashed landscapes.

The stars bleed from bad endings,

Still, they feed the dreams coming to life.

Never underestimate

How kindness can help you grow

Into the soul you were meant to be.

Every kind word puts wind in a ragged sail,

Every kind action steadies the rudder

We once thought destined for the rocks.

Embrace positive change

And use the momentum to reach your goals.

The steps you see before you

Are within reach from the right perspective,

Just believe it with your whole heart.

To the lessons I've needed,

Thank you for crushing me;

To the inspirational hearts I've held in my hands,

I am eternally grateful.

Your heartprint will forever be found

In my blessed lungs.

LAUGHTER IN THE PAIN

Sometimes I laugh when it hurts;
The tears fall
Even when I naturally
Chuckle and play it off
As if I'm not gutted,

Though I am disoriented,
Wondering what the hell just happened.
Something ending
Before its first actual breath,

Being told it's not what it was built up to be.
Those damn expectations we bury,
Trying to keep them out of sight,
Are a separate thing from having hope.

I can hold hope like a fragile Christmas bulb
Resting in my palm each morning
After I wake from a bad dream,
No matter how many times it hit the rocks.

A constant cycle,
Weary heart and brand-new eyes
Let words paint the canvas I hold,
Waiting for the picture to be slowly revealed.
And when the time is right

It will fall into place,

But not without me

Stepping up,

Reaching out,

To catch falling stars.

I have witnessed

These little glass bulbs of hope,

Luminous.

In them, my heart has been reborn.

THE BLUR

A blur from driver's side,

Color flashes then fades,

Words like confetti in a winter whirlwind;

So much to say,

Yet no way to convey the intention.

This season takes us to the brink of collapse,

Withered and frayed,

Left for the crows to scavenge.

Still, we feel the weight,

We taste the wreckage,

And we carry on through the grey landscape of life

A little lighter today.

We are on the other side of the darkest hour,

Keep the faith,

Push through the melancholy

As the days grow stronger and warmth returns.

She will always come back,

Even when words escape the pen;

There is always another chance to find

A way to say what has eluded you.

ASPEN AND EVERGREEN

Somehow, I became tangled
In the aspen and evergreen,
Working my way to sand and sun.
My stubborn Irish skin refuses to darken,
But that's okay.
I like how your golden glow
Sets a luminous gleam in your eye.
In the high plains I sit,
Scribbling words that bubble up,
Trying to erase the disconnect
My head creates...
Maybe I think too much.
I do understand how it all began,
But healing began in the fractures
Of this bruised heart.
I've heard sometimes
Things happen when you least expect
And here I wait,
Unsure of anything and
Questioning everything.
Can I give you freedom enough to be weightless,
Yet stay involved enough to be committed?
A precarious balance is needed,
As with everything in life,
Though most times we lose the joy.
We trip through an unexpected spark,
Brilliantly broken with the light
Of living through the free fall,

Devastation, and unwanted endings.

Fear of failure can bring hesitating,

Stuttering responses to every echoing heartbeat,

Tearing at the possibilities

We surrendered to fate.

BRAVER THAN I

Where are the brave ones?

The ones who howl in the daylight,
The ones who never learned to whisper,
The ones who speak with a true heart,
Not just project an illusion,
A shadow on a graffitied wall,
All bite and little bark.

I've lost my taste for my own blood;
This tongue is swollen
With all the times it's been bitten,
So now I'll take a step in faith;
Actions say more than silence ever does.

I made the choice
To ring in the New Year on unfamiliar ground;
If I do this alone for the 9th year in a row, so be it.
I'll take a chance on it all
And if it goes to hell, then *hell* is what fate intended.

Taking chances knowing you might fall
Is how you see what is meant
By no step at all.
I've landed facedown plenty of times,
But this didn't stop my heart from beating;
One time I may just fly
And make a difference in this fraying tapestry.

An open invitation without pressure
I doubt anyone will believe, but it's true;
I know what desire in a new beginning,
Nothing's ever guaranteed
Unless you hide and never reach for more,
Then you are guaranteed
To have gained absolutely nothing.

I'll buy you a drink,
Sing you a song,
Hope like hell it's the melody
You've been anticipating.
If it isn't, I'll have a definitive answer
To this beautiful ride.

Bring on the baptism by fire,
Let my ashes be my legacy,
I have nothing left to fear.

WHAT THE HEART WANTS

What do we find in this labyrinth of veins?

Valves and arteries.

A mystery most times,

What grabs these strings

Then whispers like a hurricane.

Pay attention to this,

It will change the shift of your axis;

We all have certain things

That grab us by the collar

And stand us transfixed on the subtle phrase of a note.

The way they speak,

Or say your name in a new way,

Like lightning, rips through your auditory lobe.

Your blood races,

You smile drunkenly

From then on, reading poetry in their voice,

Inflection soothing the bruises

You forgot were even there.

Maybe you build it up

To more than they intended,

But as they say,

Who can know how the heart truly works?

It's usually the small things—

How they absentmindedly play with their hair,

How they hold their breath under stress,

How they beckon you to bed after a long day,

Or pull back from you

When they're learning to grow.

You do your best not to take it personal

When you've merely been shelter in raging storms,

Perhaps you can only be temporary safety

If they choose to anchor in your harbor.

Keep your lighthouse burning bright

In the distance,

Hoping your touch is the only one they choose,

The only one they want to call home

Without the fear of judgement or rejection—

This is a place few find and even fewer hold onto.

Defy the odds,

You could make the difference.

EULOGY

Here is the eulogy of a man
Who learned things the hard way,
Made a list of mistakes
Longer than the dark sea could hide.
He was kind,
Sometimes to a fault,
Believed everyone to be truthful
When it came to love,
And found out we all have our own version
Of being honest.
Perhaps we told ourselves lies long enough
They become some twisted form of the truth.

He was lost,
Stumbling through life haphazardly,
Naive beyond belief.
He never needed to second guess
Until he was broken beyond recognition,
Only to grow from the wreckage
With bulletproof wings
Forged in the brimstone and hellfire of life.

Here he lies,
The shell of a soul once born
Into the blindness of who he truly could be
And what he might become.
In the twilight of it all
He buried what he has known,

Had gratitude for what shaped him

Into who stood here before,

Realized was time for rest.

This will be more than a new page,

New chapter,

New book—

This is a new life,

Starting with some knowledge of heartache,

A loss of innocent eyes,

And the drive to reach

For what his soul has always known.

Rest in peace, Weary Heart,

You are the fuel for the next life;

I would say goodbye,

But I know it's never really the end.

SLEEPING TREES

Sleeping trees and a power pole like a crucifix,

The day crawls from behind the frozen landscape.

My bones ache with trepidation,

Counting down the last time

I'll feel the cold blade of winter

Slip between my ribs,

Dig at my failing heart,

And leave me numb and spent.

I've always held an outdoor job;

I accept I wouldn't last a day

Inside an office fighting for air

While the constant chatter

Drained the very life from my soul.

I've chosen a solitary path

Where my thoughts can run the frigid valley

Where mountain lions watch in the distance

And the crane tree stands silent,

Patiently waiting for life to return in the spring.

There are times I feel like

The sun hesitates its ascension,

Delaying the inevitable,

Kisses our eyes with

New hope,

New perspectives,

A new chance

To make this day count for something

Something more than merely half-lived,

Half-assed,
Half-hearted.

We make what it becomes,
We choose how we are remembered:
Breaking down or breaking ground.
Resolve will carry us forward,
Perseverance will win the day.

READING PALMS

She pulls me in
As the morning paints the sky
With a blush of pink
Blending into amber coals,

Tracing constellations
In the freckles on her chest,
I am alive in her breaking light,

Transfixed by the way
Her eyes shadow
In the glow of windowpane.

Stars watching jealously,
Dimming in her rising,
She awakens to the bloom
Hidden beneath her skin.

I am sheltered in her palm
Between her life line and love line,
Cradled in salty kisses,
The pull of ocean tides.

My heart hungers for shorelines,
New moons,
Lighthouses abandoned in the modern age,

Landmarks where the world began
Inside the seeds planted in our souls,
The look of disbelief,

How we ended up here,

Burning eyes in the rising sun,

Sleepless,

Restless,

Relentless in the search

For the flavor of forever,

Unsure some days if this is even a possibility.

Yet we find a way to scrape together

Just enough hope

To press forward.

One more tattoo,

One more sign of life

In the distance;

Reach out,

I'm still right here.

Find what you need,

Feel the way we held each other

Like orphans in the wilderness

Waiting for spring to come back around.

WINTER WHEAT

Winter wheat,

Rising sun,

The stars almost put to bed,

Morning has already kissed your lips,

And I w a i t,

Searching for satellites

To spell out your name.

I had forgotten

How long one minute can be,

How time can expand

Or contract depending

On the amount of heart captured.

I should have been

On that jet

Heading to your smile,

But here I am putting wishes

On dying lights

As jet streams paint

A growing glow

On the horizon

And your eyes

On a mountain top.

I will listen for the words

This tongue has traced

On your skin,

Teeth marks

Now like faded tattoos.

Pen to paper,

Scratching down

These random,

Pointless words,

I am beginning to accept my fate,

What I've been trying to reach.

Perhaps I want more

Than I thought possible;

Maybe there's a chance

To hold a bigger dream

In these calloused hands.

Could there be something

In this picture I've missed?

Now my heart would scream, *Yes,*

Yes, there is something

That changes everything.

One thing can change a perspective,

An attitude,

The way we taste our day.

The possibility of love

Can rewrite our tangled veins

Into a symphony,

Rearrange constellations

Into memories.

Stories of how this all began

Are ever-expanding

And we are unable to see the end.

Perhaps we only need

To remain in the now

To experience life fully,

To write it all in ink,

Sketch it down,

And carve it into the walls

Of our heart,

Immortal.

WATER REFLECTIVE

I am caught in the reflection of you
And how you appear to me.
I see strength in places
You hide out of fear,
Fear of being misunderstood
Or disregarded altogether.

I see strength in knowing
You need time to heal,
Time to find out who you are,
What you really want for your future.

It is a rare heart
That searches itself for answers
Instead digging into one more lover
Or chasing one more feather.

I sit here on the shore,
Watch you move like the ocean,
Water reflective
With the power of the tide,
Drawing me in effortlessly,
Unintentionally.

I am drawn in all the same,
I am your fan,
I believe in your potential for more.
I only want to encourage you
To push through the unknown,
Discover how deep you can go.

You are limitless

Like the possibilities of chance,

And still destined for more.

Look up and see the light,

The way this all works out

As it was always meant to.

Show your world

How it looks to bloom

No matter which season

You are planted.

GHOSTS OF HOLIDAYS PAST

I may have gone too soon,

Held on too long,

Or made the perfect exit.

The stories I left you with,

Memories

Both tragic and intoxicating,

Beautiful and dark,

They are part of me,

Who I am,

Who I was,

And who people

Will come to know as me.

I have done all you said;

Some things you remember

I cannot deny or confirm,

But it is what you took

From the moments we shared.

Maybe you recall the way

The sun lit up everything,

The way the stars shimmered

When I stood up and cursed the moon,

Drunken in my despair,

Believing I would live forever.

See, I sold that lie to myself

Every day I opened my eyes,

But there was a day

I had to lay it all to rest,

Whether by my own hand

Or the hand of someone wiser than I.

Here I am on the other side,

And you miss me;

You should, because we meant something,

We touched each other's lives

Once upon a time.

Yet now you are there

And I am here;

And it hurts, as it should.

Having a piece of yourself

Taken away is painful

And difficult to process,

Live through,

Begin to resign.

But here's the thing,

Never let it steal

The time you have left,

Time is fleeting—

The most precious of possessions.

If you burn hours,

Days,

Weeks,

Months,

Years away,

Then you are losing out on *now*.

Our time should be spent

Celebrating moments,

Creating new ones;

Living this life to the fullest

Is not done lamenting ghosts.

If you want to show me

How much I meant to you,

Set your life on fire, screaming

This is how life should have been.

HER TIDE

See how the tide reacts to her smile,
How the waves break before her;

She faces the storms head-on,
Defiant in their roaring thunder;

A ripple of kindness calms
The beating beast within my chest.

Rain on her skin like sweet honey
Directly from God;

Each step brings her to the shoreline
To watch as the magic she speaks comes to life.

The power to awaken something
Once thought lost,

Something buried for a thousand years
Rising to the surface to show it never truly died,

Merely hibernated for all this time.
I will watch her wings unfold,

Soar over the fray
Where she was always meant to be...
Fly on.

CHERRY BLOSSOM SKIES

We walked the streets
Beneath a cherry blossom sky
After the rain settled
On the edge of winter's first kiss.

Bundled up in the morning's afterglow,
I could see the wheels turn inside your head,
Transfixed by how this all came to be
Here and now.

Timeless in our reverie
With a taste of fear,
The fear this is the zenith
Of our mark on one another.

How do we avoid the self-sabotage,
These landmines left from other wars,
Battles when we laid down our arms
Lifetimes ago?

In case I never said this,
You will always be a new moon to me,
When I see you in the nighttime sky
Heaven looks so much clearer.

All the distractions the full moon
Illuminates fade from my periphery;
It is you and the gateway to the universe,
A trillion stars and a celestial cloud of mystery.

PERMENANCE

I still feel your gaze
Long after the sun has risen,

The draw of your eyes
Upon the nape of my neck,

Hairs bristle with the thought of
You fresh upon my skin.

Nights are longer,
The pull is more intense,

Yet I see you in my sky
Reminding me

Of what my head starts
To doubt with the passing of time.

But my heart knows how it was moved
Beneath a sweet strawberry sunset;

Something about the late August sun
Leaves permanent marks on a soul.

The way I get lost in my daydreams,
Perhaps I am foolish enough

To think we can defy the odds
And let something bloom in the heart of wildfire.

Heal, and find your footing.

If I'm still on your mind when things settle,
We can help each other up the mountain again.

And if not, I'll still cheer you on

As I watch you ascend

On your way

To where you were meant to be.

UNRAVELING HEARTS

So many things wrapped up in this head—
My tongue tied with the dreams of angels and devils
Suspended inside the infinite.

The focus of the finite beneath a beating heart,
I find feathers in my chest,
Memories of this unraveling,

I discover the horns and thorns of what I let burn away,
Tattoos on my flesh
Of learning to live without the shackles of the status quo.

Life is a frozen exhale dissipating with the rage of winter
And it withers before our eyes like fruit left on the vine,
The unnecessary grind,

Race,

Scar,

And hollow place.

Every kiss you laid tasted of goodbye
More from fear than ceremony,
And the stars held your eyes,

Held your breath,
Held your love,

Lightyears from this fragile frame of dark and light,
Expanding since the dawn of time.

I am spent like pocket change

Sold between these lines,

A balance of what this was and what it's come to be.

Wings of white with the darkest eyes,

Halos glittering like veins of gold

Wrapped around a finger.

UNBROKEN WEIGHT

I refuse to break
With the weight of this uncertainty.

My belief in the future
Allows me to merely bend

With the winter's chill;
Deeper roots, grown in the storms of life,

Keep me from buckling
Like the world around me.

All the fragility I witness
Has me questioning what makes up my heart;

It isn't frozen,
Far from numb,

But it pushes me on
Through the devastation love has left

In the creases and buried in the folds.
Maybe I'm not wise enough to accept this demise,

Or maybe laying at rock bottom,
Broken back and withered heart,

Has built something stronger
On a cornerstone I never knew existed.

You may believe I never felt a thing,
But I've suffered in my silence;

Something you can't understand,
Since there must always be a victim

In your storyline.

Sadly, we are each the victim,
Each the offender,

Both light and darkness,
One doesn't exist without the other.

So, here I wait,
Working towards finding out

How much resilience I have left
And just how far perseverance can take me.

Celebrating the journey
That leads to breaking, and still coming up

Striding into the unknown
With blurry eyes and a heartbeat

Filled with hope and purpose.
You can never write this out of my veins.

ALWAYS IN THE EYES

And what if
Being told
It just wasn't
Meant to be,

Makes me want
To do my best
To prove
You wrong.

Perhaps
I want to take fate
By the collar
And show it

We can
Bend the light,
Turn the impossible
Into a beautiful moment,

Unimaginable.

We do have a say
In how this
All goes down.

Persevere through
The swallowing night,
Hold fast to the coming dawn.

First light will bring the comfort
Of new possibilities,

The warmth
Melts the cold,

The color comes back
To your skin,

Purpose
Settles in your bones.

You are always more
Than you give yourself credit for.

Remember this fallout,
The devastation

Handed to you blindly.
Those moments

Were there to show
Your resilience.

They left warpaint
On your soul,

Showing how you survived
The coming undone.

The seed, unrecognizable,
Blossoms into a great oak.
Embrace who you will become,

It is in the eyes,
Always in the eyes.

CAREFUL WORDS

You must be extra careful
With the words you choose
When talking to a writer,

We tend to pull apart
Every possible ounce of meaning
From the spaces between the letters.

Intent in every syllable
Magnifies the tone
Behind the shadowy light

Under which they were first spoken.

We dig our heart into the words;
Whether love or lust,
They are never taken lightly.

The only way we let go
Is when the cold blade of indifference
Pries it from our bloody palms.

Kill us with silence,
Our Achilles' heel.
Strip our skin of any color

And we will embrace the pain
Like it is the only home
We've ever known.

We sing of love and loss
Like it is the only way
To feel fully alive.

For the record,
There is no room for judgement
And no need for guilt,

This gift we were given
Is a cross we willingly bear.
It is all we know,

How we tick, so to speak,
How the blood moves
Through our veins.

You may not be immortal
In the bleeding of a pen,
But you will linger forever

In the chambers of a willing heart,
Brilliant and bruised
In the light of inspiration.

We all know you never intended
To tilt the axis of this world
Inside our souls,

But we will embrace you
Like forever
Still spells your name.

MODERN INCOMMUNICADO

I'm not looking for apologies.

Things have a way of getting sideways

In the modern age of information,

Which only lends itself

To miscommunication.

I hear the words

Read in a tone unintended,

So the cycle spirals

Into a bloody mess

And empty feeling

In the pit of my stomach,

A comedy of errors

Until we are less than strangers.

At least most of the people

I've never met

Don't make me think they hate me.

Then again, maybe

I'm just an asshole

Who can't see the truth.

It's been established

I don't listen very well,

Have a blind spot the size of Texas,

No offense.

Now I sit

Even more confused than before,

(Btw thanks to the mutual friend

Who only delivers messages

That seem to stir

Some sort of *wtf* response

In the unintended recipient).

I write to purge the mess inside my head,

This is my therapy

Aired out for the world to see,

My bloodmarks,

Shitstains, and piss buckets

Full of poor decisions.

You want a poster boy for

Fucking up a wet dream?

Look no further.

I'm known to turn a phrase,

And write a tune

That cuts right through

A perfumed whorehouse,

But I digress.

I hope you forward the message

That there is no ill

From this side of the trough,

It was a learning curve

I never quite mastered,

One I'm still trying to pass.

But fuck me for feeling,

Trying,

And actually giving a damn.

As much as I try

Not to be the nice guy,

I still am—

That isn't changing

Anytime soon.

A SORT OF RESURRECTION

I felt it
Under my ribs,

There was less space
Than I expected,

The bruising deeper
Than I realized.

Yet there are hands
With gentle fingers,

Hearts with healing beats,
Souls sent to warm

The winter from my bones.

I swallow the remedy,
Keep the secret under my tongue,

The eyes will always pull me through.
Good or bad,

I will get what I need,
It will be the framework

For the story that I tell,
Of my resurrection.

III. WATERMARKS

CHARITY

The road goes on
With or without us,

It offers us a chance
At living,

Or an opportunity
For growth.

We can run it out
Until there's no more road to run,

Find a piece of us
We never knew we missed,

Or the ember
We believed forever lost.

Either way, it's up to us
To choose

Where, and when,
How, and what.

If we let someone else
Make our choice

We will wither
In the bar ditch.

No one can live
This for us.

Push through
The broken pavement,

The path we find
On the other side will be true.

Open your heart,
Show kindness,

Never forget love is
The only cure for a broken heart,

Share that charity
Like it has no chance of running dry,

And guess what,
It will be truly endless.

HIDING PLACES

Find places
Hidden from sight,
Felt only with
The heart and soul,

Never found
On the well-worn path,
Always on
The road less traveled.

Find who
You always were,
Grow into
Your full potential...

Bloom.

A shine no one else
Has hidden
Beneath their skin,

The flash you found,
Illuminated.
A stunning version
Of the Northern Lights

Dancing above everyone
Who looks on in awe.
Embrace this step,
Press forward on this journey,

It truly never ends.
There is always
More road ahead,
New views,

Fresh horizons
To fill your dreams.
Exhale the stale,
Inhale the vibrance of truly living.

LIVING WRECKAGE

She holds secrets
In hidden places;

Things below the skin
She never talks about,
Though lives daily.

I am a hole in the drywall,
A bloody nose
That never stops throbbing,
Even in the deepest sleep.

I feel I should apologize
For not being more,
For not cauterizing
Your blood flow,
Although I never threw the blow
That caused the rupture.

I am merely the one left
Bloody in this aftermath.
I'll drink the poison,
Float a little longer
On this sea
That whispers a name
I never understood.

I simply tried to slow the stain
And swallow the riptide,
Only to wake up on a rusty shore.

Alive, not yet living,

Awake, eyes shut tight...

Until now.

Breathe,

Blink,

Break your own heart.

The world will only remember

The ones who crawled

From the wreckage of their lives.

NO FILTER, NO CHASER

Life has no filter.

It is straight,
No chaser.

You feel the burn,
Pray for the moment

When the endless blue
Smiles down on your skin.

The warmth,
The golden moments,

Slip below the surface,
Carry us through the storms,

Knowing we may
Never feel that again.

We are destined
For more sunshine than rain,

More smiles than pain,
Fluid in the way we drift

Back and forth
In the fray and feathers,

All part of the beauty
Blooming within this jagged frame.

The outside weather
Never touches the core

Of who we are,

Who we will always be.

Never forget who you are,

Hold fast to the touchstone of your soul,

It will get you through the chaos,

Bound to arise when least expected.

QUIET LIVES

Quiet lives
above bustling streets,
blue-sky days,
siren-filled nights.

She was all teeth and tongue,
Silent prayers behind dark eyes,
Dreams of a tomorrow
Beneath the ashes of yesterday.

Brilliant and bold,
Unleashed in the scattering of birds,
I have witnessed her sunrise
And held on through her sunset,

Burning beyond recognition.
My heart still beats
With the strength of raven wings,
A calm inside the storm.

What beauty blossoms
Between the cracks,
Asphalt and concrete
Cannot hold her back

From reaching for
Heaven's promise
While grounded in
The immortal sands of time.

HORIZON'S PLUME

A plume across the horizon,
Somewhere,
Someone sees your ripple;
Across the landscape,
Someone feels your intention.
Sometimes we are blind
To our own influence;

Whether we intend it or not,
We affect the world around us
With the kindness we show
Or the disdain we render.

Lives bloom in sunlight,
Souls wither when left
Too long in the dark;
Show the light,
Spread the warmth,
Push for full potential,
Make a difference.

There are enough
Heartless faces to encounter;
Be real,
Be yourself,
Know you are enough.

The ocean, she roared,
The tide, she rolled;
In that moment, I knew
my soul had changed.

There was no going back
To anything I knew before;
Nothing can remain
after being struck by a cresting wave.

We work to find our footing,
Move forward
In the name of survival;

Remembering the love
We lost in the storms
Is gone but not forgotten.

Love is always found
In the spaces between our ribs;
When we breathe, they soothe
the bruises we found in the dawn.

The pain has always been
Worth the rapture,
Even in the undoing.

EVER-CHANGING LIGHT

The river rolls,
Holding secrets
She never will tell.

Catfish dreaming
Of living life
In a wishing well,

Eyes adjusting
To the ever-changing light.

The moon spoke louder
Than my heart last night;
Listen for the silent weep,

Prayers broken in our sleep.
I could have
Said it seamlessly,

But the glass in my mouth
Needs setting free,
A shock to a system once sure.

Yesterday holds
Tomorrow's reflecting lure;
I'll never be what fits this shoe,

So take
What you feel
Can get you through.

BLOODY RAIN

I admit

I have no idea

How to love someone,

Let alone myself;

Nothing can make me

Taste my own self-loathing

Like someone attempting to love me.

I'm trying to figure out

Why this is my ritual;

I know it's not healthy,

I can see the way

It affects the world around me.

I see it all,

Yet here I am, dead.

I am numb,

Even with tear-stained cheeks,

And bloodshot eyes;

Maybe I'm certifiable.

I should lock up my empathy,

Sew it tightly shut

Away from the light of day,

Away from the damage

This jagged wreck causes.

Before you feel sympathy,

Remember, I know I am ruined;

I will cut out a piece of me for you,

Never blink,

And still be confused

Why it was never enough.

Not everyone becomes a song,

Not all of us are poems,

Some of us were born

To be a beautiful epitaph

And rest easy in this bloody rain.

PHOTOGRAPHIC FLASHBACKS

There are certain photos
That take you right back
To the captured moment.

They aren't always
Magnitude seven,
Earthshaking events

Like weddings,
Births,
Graduations,
Funerals.

Sometimes they are a simple flash,
A temporary tattoo
On a naked shoulder

In an illuminated bedroom
The morning after
No sleep the night before.

Minute glimpses of forever
Lingering a little too long,
The dusty frames in your mind.

They wash away
In the daylight
Like so many others,

Each one unique,
A differing angle
Of the same image

Becoming Monets

In the rising winds of time,

Eroding the crispness of your memories.

LONESOME FEAR

Could it be
We fear loneliness
Because of the way
We trace our own names?

Bloody and jagged,
A distorted self-portrait
When we wish to remain blind
In our busyness,

Grasping at distractions
To gild our broken reflections,
Swallowing the poison
Of our minds

Like an elixir,
When the remedy
May only be as complicated
As embracing solitude.

What if the disease is the cure
For fighting the inevitable emptiness
Where we are all surely buried
From time to time?

The surrender
And breaking of a tragedy,
The headlines for pages of prose,
Lost letters to ourselves,

Righteous in the revelry,

We succumb

To the ghosts

We were born.

FIRST TATTOO

Let's talk about your first tattoo,
The first time you embraced the pain
And let it paint your skin
With bruises and pinpricks,

Allowing the colors to settle
Just below the surface,
The bleeding of pleasure,
The subtle smile,

The rush of serotonin.
We lay swaddled
In the blush of a thousand knives,
carving our story right before our eyes.

Seductive,
But as temporary as an exhale,
We live our lives asking for more,
Filling in the shadows,

Connecting the moonlight
With a faint glowing
In the blooming horizon.
Our primal drive

Feeds the basic emotional urge
To feel something;
Anything is better than nothing,
Our first tattoo of heartache.

SLIPSTREAM CRESCENDO

Let me hear that note,

The one that breaks your heart,

The one that sets your soul on fire.

Sing like it's your chance at redemption,

Write like it's your eulogy,

Your divine epitaph.

What you will be remembered for

Is the way you were reduced to ash,

How you let the stars push through your chest.

Impact is all about how

You move the tides with your tongue,

Your fingers,

Your exhale.

Write a sacred word,

Spell the magic phrase,

Bring everything to its knees.

We will all go down together

Breathing pure oxygen,

Swallowing the honey of God's lips,

Painted cherry red,

Glowing like an Armageddon sunset.

Inspiration will rest you in its belly,

Swaddle you in blind faith,

And always find a way to resurrect you

In the final twilight.

Never give up showing you're alive,

The world will always need

A shining example of possibility.

You, my friend,

Are the pure definition—

Revelation in the darkened depths.

STORIES

I have stories,
They refuse to see the light of day.

My mother cannot understand
Where these words were born,

So she prays with words
She has mastered over her lifetime.

I have a father
Who lived these lines,

Yet locked them away
For a thousand years,

And wakes in the mask of a common man.
Oddly, I have his hands

And enough of his heart
To stumble into his footprints from time to time,

Creating my own scars with rows I've hoed,
Choices I've made.

It would seem
Something like freedom is a gift

Wrapped inside our own skin.
Until it is opened,

We are destined to carry
The burden of a stranger's sin,

The expectations
Of another's dream.

THE DISCONNECT

I am a disconnect.

Alone,

Naked,

A cold room.

I see myself hovering

Above myself.

Whitest of sheets

A tangle,

A rising wail

Far in the distance,

A dying train...

I haven't dreamed of trains

Since I was a curious child.

Perhaps this is an unfocused circle,

Moments of life,

The grand exhale,

A witness to stars,

Intersecting constellations.

Lost civilizations

Spend long nights

Drawing personal stories,

An entire mythology,

Out of exit wounds

In a bruised velvet canopy

Hung above our head.

So, the dreamers dream,

We picture life

As we hope it will be

Standing in our own myths,

Where moments of humanity and divinity

Search for strength

In our weakest parts.

It is eye-opening

How many common threads

Are found in a disconnect.

RUST AND RUBBLE

The song never started
Until she closed
Her weary eyes
After everything
She hoped to see bloom
Had been set on fire.

Every dream she awaited
Was shaken
To an unrecognizable skyline
Veiled in rust and rubble.

BURNING TEMPO

I get lost in the meter;
This tempo-driven heart
Trips on its fevered soul.

I like to feel the blush
As the tongue curves
Along the hipbone of a melody.

It seems to grin wider
When bitten lips taste
Of rusty tin razors.

The words fall as they will
In between the spaces,
The breaths stolen in silence.

We burn them like kindling,
Praying for a fire to rage,
And blood to rush, swollen in slumber,

Dreaming of eyes
We can never erase,
No matter how we try.

There will always be
A familiar shadow
In a certain light;

Flame dancing naked
Upon an empty wall
Until you no longer remember

The shade of her crescendo.

PAINT ME IN SHADOW

She paints me in fading light,
Long shadows and rusty rails.

Lines smear like lipstick and
We watch the colors bleed,

Running unrecognizable
Outlines of who I could have been.

Hands of a clock
Wrapped around my throat,

Lovingly violent and
Hazardously seductive like a bear trap,

The snare in a bed
Of peony and lavender.

Why do I dance
Into the teeth of this viper pit?

I have no answers
For how I became tangled,

A blink and a bruise
Find me shaken in my undoing.

The splintering of a hollow heart is
A storyline that fades into a foreign tongue,

A dialect with no translation,
A lost language of dreams, centuries old.

Plunged into this withering sight,
I lost the shimmering golden hue

Lifetimes ago...
I am uncertain I ever want it to return.

4:40 AM

4:40 a.m.

440.

A frequency of the modern pitch,

Tonal,

A sense of discord,

Palpable dissonance in the framework

Of this manufactured timeframe,

The consistent grinding of salt into wounds

We never knew a generation before,

Picked apart every day.

We have slipped into somberness,

Slept too well,

Too deeply,

Until our dreams blur

Our sense of depth.

The children born of the disconnect,

Fed on fear and loneliness,

Standing in the shadow, skinless,

Broken like the teeth of a shaken poet.

A madman, trembling in his thoughts

Because he never tasted honey,

Salivating in a kind of bitterness

That burns the tongue,

Waters the eyes,

Is swallowed like glass,

Unrepentant,

Justified

In his own fury.

MOVING PICTURES

How did we dream
Before moving pictures?

How did our nocturnal scenes roll out?
Were all the characters

Possibly
Played out like Shakespeare,

Bad actors and sad actresses?
Did anyone look at the world in black and white

Still frames
Before the first camera was revealed?

Did the dawn of man
Begin in darkened, dreamless sleep,

Sabertoothed nightmares,
Mammoths trampling our reverie?

I have a difficult time believing
There haven't always been dreams

As I witness the progress,
Some may argue the digress, of mankind.

Perhaps dreams have always been
Played out like movie scenes,

We merely had nothing
To compare,

Or perhaps movies have always been
What dreams were trying to be.

AVERAGES

To never feel
More than average,

Like everyone's perception
Has some sort of value
Outweighing your own.

It is a travesty
To lose your identity
In the tidal wave of words

The world
(A world with overinflated self-worth)
Showers down upon you.

They will leave you torn,
Half-alive in the echo
Of your own heartbeat.

A voice built for surging tides,
And shifting seasons,

You are more than their jaded perceptions.

A LIFETIME AGO

A lifetime ago
When things weren't so jaded,
I had the pleasure of being
Dizzy and star-crossed.

I threw my heart around
Like it was immortal,
Patched it up
With a little twine,
And hoped for a better day.
I would dust it off,
Use it for a battle shield.

As the years drunkenly stumbled by,
There was less and less to repair.
I slowly traded passion for apathy,
My heart became unraveled
Until I no longer felt at all.
The stopping and starting
Caught up and left me with empty hands
And an empty chest.

LIMBO

Limbo, the surreal space
Between heaven and hell,
Has nothing to torment you,
Yet has no sense of rapture.
Fighting complacency
Without a sense of purpose,
Digging deep for positivity
While trying to make a difference.

Neither darkness in your sky
Nor any form of light
Merely take life as it comes.

Live in the *now*,
Avoid the wreckage
You pass daily
While helping fellow travelers
Back onto the road.
Be caring and loving
Without the trappings of
Being *in* love.
Learn to love life,
Accept moments
Less than dramatic.

GOLDEN LEDGES

Hold your breath...

l

  e

   a

    p

From the golden ledge
Where you have precariously perched
For longer than intended.

You must be blind to your wings
And that your instinct to fly
Will rescue you from the rocks below.

A comfort zone
Is but a gilded coffin,
Quiet and cold.

We bury ourselves
In excuses and half-truths,
An attempt to make life safe;
Accepting that a bird in the hand
Is a default of winning.

Seize hold of your trajectory,
Aim higher,
Shoot farther.
The prize is limitless
If you are willing
To let go of what you believe
Your world is built upon.

TARNISHED HALOS

I never intended
To tarnish your halo,

Simply witness the shimmer of your horns
Like city lights off your lower back

Through that fifth story window
Without a star in sight.

Your sweat was the Milky Way,
A reverse negative

Examined in a dark room,
Anything but silent

In 3D exploration
Lost in the war of life.

Casualties count down the sands
Steadily sifting through the hourglass,

Numerous as the goosebumps
Along your belly and across your chest.

Labored breathing caught
In a disheveled bed,

Lamenting dawn and returning to everyday steps
We tried to wash from our path.

There was never an escape,
Merely a suspension of routine;

Taking the long way home

Only to find a memory of the house once sacred

Is now a stranger's bedpost.

Another's tattoo on your skin

A reminder of the hidden halo

Only meant to be held while sin was on your tongue.

IV. TIDAL

SILENT MEDIOCRITY

A powerful mirage
Built to keep you like a rat in a cage
Under the thumb of the heartless,
The ones with souls less than pristine,
The evil arisen to rule cruelly.
Every heart that beats,
Every mouth that hungers
For something better than they have known before
Is a bootheel on the neck of the hopeful,
Whatever it takes to drive the helpless to desperation.

Quiet desperation isn't built for your ending;
You require more than the silence mediocrity creates.
A dull murmur lost in another lifetime
When another generation does not remember your name,
Your voice, or the way you begged for the darkness to swallow you,
And hold you in its belly like the seed of Cain.
The spark of life in the valley of the shadow of death
Where in the shepherd was found
Was nothing but a snake oil salesman
Who has sold you for a handful of silver.

Exhale your last prayer in candlelight,
Search for the ear of a god
Who only hears a solitary voice,
Answering only if you speak Latin
And dress in a sacred cloth,
Rent from top to foot.
I write from a blind spot,

The echo isn't what I hoped it would be,

Yet here I am, Cheshire grin and whisky breath,

With these things listed as sins

I dare to speak beyond my knowing.

Do not misinterpret my words;

There are things grander than we who live in broken silences,

We who can feel the ebb and the flow of a universe.

The sky is far too high,

The ocean so deep

We speak with tongues stained with our father's sins,

Our mother's lost innocence,

How we can never return to where we once were

When we first tasted the blade of our own humanity.

A ROOM HALF-FAMILIAR

Startled awake by an echo,

He opens his heavy eyes

To a room half-familiar,

Illuminated with dim light

Seeping through

Tightly closed blinds.

He finds his way through cobwebs of thought,

Blurry and confused,

Trying to shake

The sleep

From his unfocused vision.

Turning his head towards the nightstand,

He peers past a silent choir of empty bottles

To the clock reading 10:13 AM.

In his mind

He hears

An off-key meadow lark

In the kitchen singing her own melody

For *Good Day Sunshine*.

She will never not be an angel

Preparing for the day to begin

Inside those soft yellow walls,

Standing before a 1970s yellow oven.

Heat rises from the stove top,
Perhaps she never believed it would ever get
any

    better

        than

            this...

Prepping breakfast for a man
So wrapped up in his own jagged dreams
Of lust, while counting down
To the first beer of the day.

The oatmeal steams in a Corning bowl
On a round, white laminate dining table.
Hot black coffee,
Slip-on work boots,
Long-sleeved, plaid, pearl-snap shirt
Over a white t-shirt,
Blue jeans,
Brown belt;
His thick dark brown hair
Combed through with Wildroot
In a habitual part from right to left.

A mood
Something like unsatisfied choices,
Not quite regret,
Lingers after he closes the door
Leading to the driveway,

A door with the imprint of a bootheel

Next to the handle,

From a night he wasn't welcomed home

With open arms

After long hours

Spent escaping the world he built.

He leaves in his white company truck

For an office where he nurses his heart

And pounding head

While searching for a way

To not return home for good.

Once he pulls away,

She exhales,

A moment of silence

Before the gentle song begins again.

Holding her own rhythm,

Finding her own melody,

Her mind grips a resolve

That one day...

She will escape this life.

Note by note

Drifting down

The darkened hallway,

Floating into a young boy's room

Where he lies

Lucid,

Dreamless,

An old lone soul

Inside baby blue walls,

A strange cliche of the nuclear family
About to feel the fallout.

Next door to the boy
His sister in a rose-pink room
Asleep in her bed,
Dreaming of something bigger than she could ever say,
A flower's bloom that grows up,
Moves eight thousand miles away
Only to find the sins of their father will follow.

As the scene fades into the darkening grey
Of yet another rainy morning,
The son, now grown, thinks to himself, "It's too damn early
to be thinking this damn much."

Moments and memories are
t
  i
    d
      a
        l to him now...

He accepts he holds no power over the ocean
Or the falling sky outside the drawn shades,
His melancholy smile creases his whitening temples,
His eyes pool to the shores of his eyelids,
He has learned how to fortify his dammed-up border.

Swallow hard,
Guide the overflow
Into the bottomless reservoir
Deep inside his aging chest.

He slips his feet into a tattered pair of slippers,

He wanders to the kitchen,

He makes a large cup of coffee,

And begins another reflective day.

WAR RANT

War is the manifestation of Cain's story,
A bludgeoning of your fellow man
Out of your own greedy heart
For no other reason
Than hatred of your own inadequacies.

War is hell,
Unspeakable things happen
And are hidden throughout the campaign
In unmarked graves of countless innocent
And less-than-innocent alike.
Blood spilt for no real gain,
Lives destroyed,
Cities left in ruin,
And survivors left to rebuild their lives
From the ground up.

Why would there be any need to sensationalize
Or enhance the devastation?
What possible reason is there
To make war seem worse than it already is?

If you haven't seen and felt something
Not quite right with the world
Over the last few years,
Let alone over the last twenty,
Then you are either completely blind
Or you choose the dark.
This mental electric shock therapy

Propagated though the entire globe

Is absolute insanity.

We have been fed false and fake images,

Videos, and a series of bad actors over and over again.

I must believe and hope against all odds

That citizens are finally waking up

To the manipulation we have swallowed

Gladly our entire lives.

The revolving illusion of evil monsters

And invisible boogey men

With no real evidence besides

What a group of people,

Paid questionably,

Say is the truth.

"Truth" was compromised a century ago

And has been in a constant state of decay ever since.

We are continuously bombarded

With the next big event to cause fear,

Loss of reason, and common sense.

Explain to me, if you will,

What possible reason is there

To use blatant lies

When reporting what is going on in this world?

Once you lie you can never truly be trusted,

Yet millions of people still trust those

Who lie directly to our faces

Every day and every night.

I refuse to drink the Kool-Aid;

I am no longer taking a pill

Or being manipulated by emotional terrorism.

My heart feels for the ones caught in their grip,

I hope your eyes open

And you begin to see the reality around you.

I beg you to stop being fodder

For the machine tormenting your mind.

Every malevolent idea

Born from the minds of evil men

At the turn of the 19th century,

Has been absorbed

Into this great country of ours

Until we are sick and dying from the inside out.

We are created for kindness,

Compassion, and love,

But those virtues are now twisted

And hyper-stimulated at a fevered pitch

That cannot be maintained.

This is the root,

How so many people we love

Are brought to mental and emotional exhaustion.

This is not caused by your fellow man,

But is perpetrated by malevolent men

Who try to rule us, not represent us.

A divided population can never fix anything,

We need to find our common ground

And work from there.

We all have more common ties

Than we have differences,

My prayer is you see behind the dark curtain

We have too long accepted as part of life.

PERCEPTIONS

I have lost hold of
What I thought to be real...

Real, as a perception.

The further the taillights fade,
The faster I attempt to run;
A longer stride
Only to wither sooner.

I've wilted before
In the growing heat of summer
When I once believed in immortality.
Self-delusion is
The common factor in every derailment.

Having a heart
With short-term memory loss,
The road seems familiar

With a sense of déjà vu.
The impending sense of fear
Never arrives.

I march to the precipice,
Blind as a newborn.

Blue skies
And silver-lined clouds
Draw me forward.

FREEFALL

The gentle wind changes direction,
I find myself in freefall

With wings too frail to hold me.
Skin too thick to care,
I forget to brace for impact,

Fresh scars, and fractures.
Bloody and blinking,
Believe I am still alive.

Time and again,
Here I remain
Without a needless resurrection,

Love cannot kill this bulletproof heart.

She wanted me to notice;
Sadly, she showed up
A lifetime too late.

PHOTOGRAPHS

Like photos out of focus,
We capture moments in our lives.

Lost in the framing,
Colors fade as details blur,
We believe in the wide angle
Panning moment-to-moment.

Slaves to our own blinded hearts,

Half-alive until the transcendent afterglow
Rests on our skin
Like heaven's dew,
Crystalline,
Shimmering.

Silver or technicolor,
The collected albums fray
The passing of time,

Fearless.

Restlessly leaving us
To squint at the panoramic,
Questioning the lapsing timeline.

Some days are black and white
Or the shade of a sepia-stained Tuesday afternoon,

Jagged shadows,
Adjacent angles,
Hues of lives once lived,

Never the same
After love leaves town.

The changing curve of our name
In the mouth of a new lover,
Unrecognizable to a portrait
The mirror sells us.

The theory of three images,
The trinity, perhaps:

Who we see ourselves to be,
Who others believe they see,
Who we really are.

The balance of the triad
Makes it nearly impossible
To pin ourselves
Beneath an under-glass display.

Evolve or die,
Stagnation is a sure path to decomposition,
An acidic demise
For an unfulfilled soul,

A life left undeveloped
On the floor of a darkroom,
Too frightened by
Should have,
Could have,
Would have
Been,

Opening our eyes to the reality we created.

HONEYDEW SKIN

She somehow
always found a way to leave
Just before the rain came,

Like a sixth sense
To avoid the fallout.

Honeydew skin,
Veins blue as her eyes,
No signs of scars
With the naked eye.

She refused to let anyone
Close enough
To see the fractures,

The splintering of lung and bone.

Stand on her shore,
Brave enough in the coming dawn
To see beneath the veneer
Where her beauty lingered.

The trouble came
When you tried to trace
The tender places,

The satiable hunger.
Heart like a flare gun
On a moonless night

Caused the closing
Of her eyes,
Her mouth

Left with empty hands,
A broken dream.

Don't let it break you,
Fight through the pangs,
The feeling of your ribs
Rubbing against your lungs.

A tidal wave of confusion
Will recede with the waning moon.

In the waxing
Life will return, shifted
With the morning light,
A sleepy glow,
Shrouded,
Redemptive
In the passing numbers.

Day one is always tragic,
Day six hundred thirty-seven, mosaic.
The pieces no longer fit the same
As the day after or the day before,

Inconclusive,
Congestive heart failure.

HAZY AND CRISP

On days like today,
Hazy and crisp with late autumn's bite,

I remember you
A little more vividly.

The lens of life refocuses
From the passenger-side window,
a blur.

I reflect on my hope that
You would be
My crackling hearth
In a difficult winter.

The complication of a growing darkness
Outside my steamy window and in my mind's eye,

You were meant to be a warm down comforter,
A shelter through the hard December storms.

The ache of brittle bones and
The itch of summer scars remain
Years after the watermarks receded.

We were less than strangers, Honey,
Lost in the city landscape,

Winter's slate was welcome
Beneath concrete and steel.

The blue tint grew
In the blinding golden foliage,

I still relive our exhaled farewell
Time and time again.

Perhaps the coming holidays and
My struggles with gratitude are
A summary of another ash-filled year.

I know I loved you
As much as I knew how to love,
Given without expectation.

Here, on the fading side of the equinox,
I'm worn down and in need of rest
My heart can never fully embrace,

No matter how hard I press into your memory.

TELL ME

"Tell me one thing you remember about me," she said.

My answer came a little too slow,

With each passing second

Every word would be a bigger lie in her ears,

As if it was a given I would fabricate a tolerable reply.

That was all she ever knew,

Stories to sedate her misgivings.

Family,

      Friends,

           Lovers.

All with the common thread:

Spoon-feeding her what they each believed

She wanted or needed to hear.

To her mind,

How could I be cut from

Any other cloth?

I took her face in my hands,

Gently put my lips to hers,

Looked her squarely in the eyes,

And told her, "If I only tell you one thing,

It will blossom into a forest of wildflowers,

Innumerable.

I need you to stay focused

On my eyes the whole time

So you can see what an honest heart looks like.

Once you begin to look, you will be unable

To turn your gaze. You will become
Transfixed by the sound of each syllable
Rolling from my tongue."

I began, "The one thing I can never forget is the collision,
The way time slowed when we intersected,
Two souls strong enough to shift an axis,
A merging rotation left this galaxy with a new orbit,
Fresh constellations with mythology yet to be written,
Yet to be dreamt.
Eyes closed in the climax of creation,
You were the sweat on my chest, the echo of a voice
In search of a home long given up.
Yet there you were,
A flame, a magnet with no way to avoid attraction;
We knew the consummation was inevitable,
How everything after would never be the same.
The search for new cliches might strike closer
To the truth we felt, closer to the heart of the moment.

You see, *one thing* rippled into a lifetime.

Events continue to shift the shoreline our feet found,
Bracing for the coming storms as the tidal rhythm
Swayed through our bloodstream and adjusted our heartbeats,
Synchronistic and sacred.
I am still drifting in your centrifugal current
Though I am a lifetime from where
This all began. I remember every drop of rain you anointed
On my skin, my tongue, my lungs,
Forever grateful I was shaken from my slumber."

SHADOWS REMAIN

You can leave the window open
And all the doors unlocked,
She will only stay as long
As she can handle the storm.

Once she sets her heart adrift
It will be nothing but
A blur of seascapes and grey horizons.

She sinks her teeth into the night,
Her feet as solid as the shore.

She isn't yours to have or even hold;
She will hold herself like the Savior in
A dream only she can feel,
Only she can love.

Speak up, but don't expect a reply;
She will be as subtle as an axis shift
Bringing summer to a close,
Winter to life.

Keep your eyes open
For the brilliant colors of her autumn.
Her chill is long gone,

Only shadows remain.

SOLITUDE

I have come to accept my soul is built on solitude,
Once heavy-handed, it is now a restless slumber.

Awakened by the rattling fog
And questions with unending answers,

I cradle my longings
With the sobering realization

Forever is merely the view from a roadside diner.
I will never finish washing the shroud you left
Hanging from the window of my lungs,

So I sink a little deeper
Into the curving shadows

Contrived with dim lights and the slight of heart.
I have no doubt you felt the quivering firmament,

The barometric pressure inside my skull,
A series of broken locks to rooms without a view.

Simply moving pictures of goodbye
Made by water-colored hands,
Moments too blurry to describe,
Too distant to name,

Time withers and is lost.
Constructed on wasted breath
With exhausted motion and motives,

We bow to the weight
We ourselves have created.

We swallow and digest
A drop of poison for the sickness,

We embrace what was lost,
What cannot be rescued

From the eternal flame of mounting history.

We focus in attempts to not squander
The vaporous youth we find ourselves passing through

As seconds turn to years,
Unaccountable for our lack of desperation
In the face of a coming end.

SINGING BIRDS

All these birds
Singing for the sun to rise,

A chorus held as dawn arrives
With dreamcatchers in their throats.

To capture a star and
Make a wish in the well of time.

They bleed together in a fevered reverie,

Desperation in the unsteady grey horizon
A blurred, three-line catchphrase laudanum.

A little something for the half-awake masses
Awaiting the next fifteen-second clip,

Messianic insta-rice
With a resonant echo of the familiar.

Plagiaristic, if may I be so bold.

Yet here you are,
Feet dangling from the rooftop,
Leaning into the summer storm,

Pen in hand,
Reaching for a lightning bolt
To cauterize your veins.

Bleeding upon this page
Namelessly,
Blamelessly bold and
Still shaken by your insecurity.

You can rest assured
The juice will be worth the squeeze.

Stay the course with seeded faith,
A fertile heart...

The taste of copper in your mouth.

SULLEN PIRATE DAYS

After a long week of sullen days
I forgot how good a clear sunrise feels,

How a sky-blue sky holds my attention
For an entire cup of morning coffee.

Lazy reminiscence about other endless blues
Spark my heart back to a childhood moment,

Precariously perched at the highest point
Of our backyard tree,

Imagining myself a pirate in the crow's nest,
Swaying in the unrelenting Wyoming wind,

Which gave the sensation of the rolling sea
I only dreamed about,

A diligent lookout for enemy ships
Or the slightest sign of land to pillage,

Keeping a keen eye out
For opportunities of bounty,

The treasure of legends,
Of dreams coming true.

One part explorer, two parts gypsy
With a hunger for travel,

Adventure and an appetite larger
than eyes can hold,

Hands born for the temporary
The way sand and water slips between fingers.

There are memories,
Moments I attempt to hold, yet never keep;

Sooner or later, the shine fades away,
The pirate sinks his ship in grandeur or in shame.

We take for granted the blue,
The warmth, the resonant.

The sun shines on every dog's ass eventually,
or something to that effect;

I often get quotes like that twisted.
I blame my mother,

Who's one of the greatest misquoters
I have ever known, much to my amusement and adoration;

She somehow kept this pirate alive
Through many an attempt to go out in a blaze of glory.

As I soak up the warm January sun,
I reflect on my journey since those days,

I see a lot of common threads.
And who knows, maybe

I'm still working towards
A pirate's end.

STALE COFFEE

I remember you looked tired,
Spent, in fact,

Like love was a lifetime
Of graveyard shifts
In late December rain.

Survival depended on how
The breaking would come,

An unraveling to the core
Of what we built,

Words we used for a wire hanger
Instead of keys to open the car,

Still running,
Breath held for a clean getaway.

But clean is in the cards
Rarely in the living,
And only hoped for in the dying.

I still picture you sitting
In that strange dark chair,

Immaculate, yet distant,
Like your heartbeat

Was in the apartment down the hall,
Or folded into the mail slot next to the elevator

In the four-story building
With an address we never remembered

No matter how hard we tried
To etch it into our skin.

Every shade of winter
Is trapped inside these shoes;

I've given up by now
And accept it will never end well.
It will never end well,

Not with this weathered heart,
Not with this ragged soul,

Road-weary and headstrong
Like stale coffee the morning after.

SOMEONE ELSE'S HANDWRITING

I have been here ten thousand times,
I accept the reality
I have less than ten thousand more;

A strange room,
An unfamiliar bed,
And an evolving mirrored perspective.

The road wears on a sole,
And my soul is
A stranger among strangers

Who become estranged.
Doors revolve,
Wheels grind on tar-papered gravel,

I drive blind into the pre-dawn darkness,
Watching the miles left in the tank
Wither and shrink
Until the alarm sounds, signaling low fuel.

I pull into a station
With bloodshot eyes and a head full of stories
That no one will ever hear.

These are the memories
That have no translation
For any other heart but mine.

I bathe in them mile after mile,
I let them settle on my skin
Like holy ashes of communion,

A retreat into solitude.

Here I stand once again, a blur,

Replaying this storyline,

Imagining the lives I've already lived,

The deaths from which I've awoken

Along this crooked path.

Sweet charity has smiled on this man's face,

My faith has been tested

Until the last grain of sand was all to be found.

Yet hope,

Hope has always been entwined in my spine,

Sending whispers of songs

To keep the wind at my back,

Pushing me further along my path,

In and out of lives I've both loved and lost,

Both a blessing and a curse

That sometimes refuses to reveal itself

Until years later when it reads

Like someone else's handwriting.

EXIT WOUNDS

I once believed the timestamp of entry
Was how watermarks were etched;
A splintering,
The moment,
A chiseling,
Temple walls in decay.
The only certainty
The spark of a catastrophic end
Foreseeing the fall of Rome.

Serpentine prayers of smoke sway,
Eyes closed with the eclipse of time.
My axis shifting,
My ideology
In transition. The theory
Of what molds my perspective has
More to do with exit wounds.
Goodbyes settle into my marrow,
The pulse of a bitten tongue,
A split lip in thundering silence.
Yes, the bloody exhale
Of incalculable forgotten farewells
Ranges from pinholes to caverns;
The whistle and click of raw power,
A freight train of loss.
Unstoppable.
Inescapable.

We are each destined for a future of fading skylines.

We grasp the tumbling pieces with bloody fingertips,

Our scarred palms sculpting storylines of our pasts

From shadowed flesh and toned skin.

Sometimes memories are in black and white.

Romantic disconnect and

Poetic freefall

Try to keep our eyes open

To what will never return.

We need not lament the path we never chose.

Embrace how trajectory intersects our hearts,

Our cigarette-stained lungs

Struggling for words

A beautiful reminder

Of how we are still standing,

Surviving another empty ricochet

As the world around us continues to turn.

THE PUNISHMENT

If you want to punish me,
You are going to have to
Hit me like you mean it.

If you are looking for a way to
Fuck this all up,
You'll need to kiss me to kill it.

Shake it all to its foundation,
Never worry about the aftermath.

Whatever is left beneath the rubble
Will find the light of day
A thousand years from now

By eyes and ears with absolutely
No frame of reference
For how it all ended,

How this garden was swept into the ocean,
An anointing of sediment,
A veil of swaying sand off a lover's feet,
The dance of swept-aside memories,

Salty brine sealed in a watery tomb.
My Dear, if you are unafraid of a cataclysmic demise,
Then I am here until this current
Carries me away to another bloody sunset.

BURNING VEINS

The moon is a sliver,
An ember glowing
Through silken clouds.

I have found her
Burning beneath my skin
With thoughts of you.

She is a scar,
A cancer to these eyes,
These veins.

There are times I wish
I never laid eyes on you.

Yet, I have, and I did,
And now I'm here in the darkness
Of what is left over.

Every inadequacy turns
Like the ground beneath my feet,

Knowing I gave all I had, though
Crude and poorly expressed
Until after the fall.

I will sit here swaddled in solitude,
Digging at the pieces of you
Left in me,

Attempting to sever thoughts
From my heart,
Still bruised from the aftermath.

HEAVY BEAUTY

Late in the day,
Thousand miles behind me,
A million more to go.

On a lightless evening
The sky was close enough to caress
And meander down falling hills.

I felt her before my eyes ever soaked in her silhouette,
A row of steeples imprisoning my view
And drawn to a feeling with no explanation.

The iron in my blood was called home,
She was darkness, sweet,
Spreading across the horizon.

Speechless in swallowing silence,
A stillness born internal,
I am home but wearing a stranger's face.

The water is my ethereal soul twin,
She watches me, lost as a lamb;
I heard her voice before my birth.

Reborn in my baptism,
Lingering questions settle in her hiding places,
Kissed by a heavy beauty,

My golden thread.

PARKING LOT IN THE RAIN

The show has ended,

The last note released

Into the chasm of the liquid night above me.

Everything is packed up and loaded,

Awaiting the next night's show.

This is the moment a cigarette would be

Slid from the hard pack

While I stand beneath a parking lot light.

The rain cascades down around me

In a low, hissing static.

Picture a movie scene where

The solitary character stands

Shrouded in an off-white aura,

Glistening in a vacuumed atmosphere.

Not the sound of a bird,

A rolling tire,

Or a revving engine,

Can break the monotone sizzle

Surrounding his colorless silhouette.

His hat sags with the weight of the water

As it builds on the crown and brim,

His long hair matted to his neck and back of his shirt,

Features unrecognizable to the naked eye,

Face buried in shadow,

Upper body swelling

Then retracting with each sighing breath.

He's searching the scene

For something beyond the light's reach.

His eyes peer into the shades of black

Towards the ancient river.

Out beyond the stoic cottonwoods,

The moving water whispers a harmony

To the rain's rising crescendo.

Motionless, save his inhale and exhale,

Someone might say he is soaking in the day's events,

Carving each dripping moment

Into the granite of his aging spine.

Being drenched from sole to fingertip

Has become a ritual with water,

The physical anointing of a universe

That has beckoned him since birth

From raindrop to river to the inevitable sea,

Where we will all come to eventually rest.

ACKNOWLEDGEMENTS

I would first like to thank my daughter Laurynn, who inspires me to be a better writer. She's introduced me to authors who have helped me evolve into the writer I am today. I have no doubt one day my writing will exist in her shadow. Continue to grow and push yourself, I love you.

Thank you to my friends and family who continue to encourage me in my endeavor to make writing my livelihood. Your kindness and love mean so much more than I could ever express.

To everyone who took a chance and purchased my first book, *In The Details*, thank you from the bottom of my heart. I hope this collection will expound upon what I started.

To my fellow wordsmiths, thank you for inspiring and pushing me to step beyond my hesitancy and put these words out into the world. We all need the fire stoked from time to time, and I have some amazing souls who do that for me daily.

Thank you to the intimate ones who brought these words out from places I never knew existed. Although the phrases aren't always brilliantly painted, they had a life of their own as they found their way to the page. These pages would have been blank without your fingerprints on my soul.

ABOUT THE AUTHOR

Thomas Hinds is a father of three. He has spent the last few years as a troubadour, traveling across the country playing both his own songs and those that shaped his personal style. He released his first book of poetry and prose *In The Details*, in 2020. This collection showcased his flair for painting a scene with his words, as well as his individualized approach to expressing the common laments we all have. Whether loss or love, tragedy or triumph, Thomas brings you into a life he has lived.

He spent his formative years in central Wyoming before moving to northwest New Mexico with his mother and sister. Spending his youth in jagged, wide open spaces shaped Thomas's point of view and helped him see the world through eyes of a dissonant landscape, which still influences his unique perspective.

Thomas started writing his thoughts in first grade, mostly creating storylines for the cartoons he drew in his free time at school. In junior high, he found a voice with his pen by scribbling poetry on scraps of paper during church, which he would type up on his old Royal Travel Typewriter late in the evenings. Over the last several decades, Thomas has found a style that is his own, and yet echoes writers who have come before him. Always from the heart and as raw as it gets seems to be his way of getting everything out.

In addition to his poetry, Thomas is also an accomplished songwriter who has released two full length CDs, *Ghosts and Lamentations* (2015) and *Resurrection Road* (2019), as well as an EP titled *Barbwire Bouquet* (2017) and a single release of his song *Luminous* (2020).

Thomas is currently working on his follow-up album to *Resurrection Road*, to be released in 2022. It will coincide with the release of *Ghost of a River*. He has also started creating with physical media in the form of sketching and painting. Thomas looks forward to getting back out on the road this year and visiting old friends, as well as making new ones.

You can find more info on Thomas and his work at www.thomashindsmedia.com.

Please leave a review for any of Thomas's material, and he hopes to see you soon.

"Scars are simply roadmaps of where we've been."
Thomas Hinds

www.ingramcontent.com/pod-product-compliance
Lightning Source LLC
Chambersburg PA
CBHW020252130626
46549CB00005B/2190